Susan Canizares
Pamela Chanko

Scholastic Inc.
New York • Toronto • London • Auckland • Sydney

Acknowledgments

Early Childhood Consultant: Ellen Booth Church

Literacy Specialist: Linda Cornwell

Design: Silver Editions

Photo Research: Silver Editions

Endnotes: Sabrina Jones

Endnote Illustrations: Ruth Flanigan

———————————————

Photographs: Cover: Paul Stover/Tony Stone Images; title page: Paul Stover/Tony Stone Images; p. 1: (tl) Teake Zuidema/The Image Works; (tr) Tom Raymond/Tony Stone Images; (bl) Mike McQueen/Tony Stone Images; (br) Michele & Tom Grimm/Tony Stone Images; p. 2: Ron Sherman/Tony Stone Images; p. 3: Eastcott-Momatiuk/The Image Works; pp. 4, 8: B. Daemmrich/The Image Works; p. 5: Dave Schiefelbein/Tony Stone Images; p. 6: Gay Bumgarner/Tony Stone Images; p. 7: C. Gatewood/The Image Works; p. 9: Tony Freeman/Photo Edit; p. 10: F. Rangel/The Image Works; p. 11: Gordon Gainer/The Stock Market; p. 12: A. Ramey/Photo Edit.

Library of Congress Cataloging-in-Publication Data
Canizares, Susan, 1960-
Signs / Susan Canizares, Pamela Chanko.
p. cm. -- (Learning center emergent readers)
Summary: Photographs and rhyming text show how signs can be used to provide important messages.
ISBN 0-439-04608-4 (pbk. : alk. paper)
1. Signs and symbols--Juvenile literature.
[1. Signs and symbols.] I. Chanko, Pamela, 1968- . II. Title. III. Series.
P99.C277 1999
302.23--dc21   98-46871
                                                                                       CIP AC

10   08   03   02

Signs can tell you . . .

Where you are.

Where things go.

When to stop.

Too much snow.

Not to fish.

Not to walk.

Not to swim.

QUIET...
(please...)

Not to talk.

Where to turn.

Where to eat.

Where to find a special treat!

SIGNS

All around us, bright, bold signs catch the eye. Their messages are short and quick to read for people on the move. They help us find our way to new places. They warn us to beware of danger. They tempt us with good things to buy and eat. Signs can be put up by the government, a business, or a private person.

Peachtree Street Street signs are put up by the city to show us the way. They need to last a long time outdoors, so they are made of strong metal with baked enamel paint that won't fade in the sun. The letters are clear and easy to read. Street names can also tell you about the history of a place. Maybe a peach tree used to grow where we now see a busy city block.

Recycle area Signs at the recycling area tell us where to put old bottles and cans to be crushed, melted, and made into new ones. Paper products go into a different bin. Recycling is more complicated than just throwing everything away, but if we follow the signs we can keep our world a beautiful and healthy place to live. The signs have the special recycling symbol, which is also on plastic containers that are recyclable.

Stop This school crossing guard uses a movable stop sign to keep students safe in busy rush-hour traffic. Because he holds out his sign only when children cross the street, drivers notice it more than a sign or light that is always there. The drivers must obey this little boy because of his official sign!

Avalanche area This sign on a road barricade warns drivers of the danger of avalanches. An avalanche happens when so much snow falls in the mountains that it all slides downhill, blocking roads and burying things. The barricade keeps cars off the road, and the sign explains why. Travelers must find another road or another means of transportation.

No fishing This painted wooden sign was probably posted by the owners of the land. They want to warn others against fishing from their pond. Perhaps the fish need time to grow up and have more little fish before they can spare any!

Don't walk The "don't walk" sign flashes red to keep us from crossing into dangerous oncoming traffic. When the traffic light for cars changes to red, the "walk" sign will automatically light up. Traffic signs that warn of special danger are usually orange, because it is an alarming color.

No swimming This sign orders us not to swim in a lake. It could be for our own safety, because there is no lifeguard. Some mountain lakes are reservoirs that supply a city with drinking water. By not swimming in them we help keep the water pure.

Quiet please The "quiet" sign on a library shelf is a reminder not to talk too loudly in the library. The picture shows us why: Somebody is trying to study!

One way/detour When one sign points in one direction and another one points the opposite way, which way should we go? The "one way" sign shows the regular route, but "detour" signs are just for special situations. They guide us around an unusual obstacle, like construction, road repair, or an accident. When the road crews mark a detour, we follow the detour sign instead of the everyday signs. The special detour signs are also usually orange, because it catches the eye.

Diner Diner signs are often big and flashy so hungry travelers can see them from far down the road. The letters are cut out of metal and plastic, with electric wires running through to light them up. The glowing sign makes it look like a cheerful place to stop at night.

Donut Hole The funny shape of this sign tells us that there are fun things to eat inside. The sign is shaped just like a doughnut, which is this shop's specialty. You can go right through the hole of this Donut Hole sign!